CONTENTS

Copyright © 2024 by Sarane Hydara
All rights reserved. No part of this book may be reproduced in any manner
whatsoever without written permission except in the case of brief quotations
embodied in critical articles and reviews.
First Printing, 2024

Dedication

All corrupt Humans and human being shall read their corrupt practices and corrupt being in this book. This book is dedicated to all those who choose to change and stand on the moral high ground, desist from corrupt practices or corrupt being after reading this book and start adding value to their life, marriage, family, community, institution or nation.

REDEFINING CORRUPTION FOR HUMAN DEVELOPMENT

SARANE HYDARA

Beginning

A Ouzou Billaahi Mina Shaytani Rajeem
Bismillaahi Arahmanin Araheemin

REDEFINING CORRUPTION FOR HUMAN DEVELOPMENT

Disclaimer

This Book or the Author is not referring to any individual, group, institution or government. The Author only expressed his knowledge of corruption. Any characterisation or labelling of individuals based on the knowledge expressed in this Book its not the responsibility of the Book nor the Author.

Acknowledgement

I whole heartedly recognised the support and encouragement received from my wives, loving children. I am grateful to those who took their time to review draft copies of this book.

I am happy to mention Mr. Alpha Conteh an English teacher at Janet BSSS for reviewing this book for grammar and spellings, I enjoyed using Reedsy website to engage Vaneesa Cook as my expert Development and Copy Editor. Thankful for adding value to this book with her brilliant suggestions.

I highly appreciate Microsoft Bing for my internet research and Grammarly App. for some of the corrections done in this book.

CHAPTER 1

Preface

During my career as a civil servant in the Gambia, as a procurement officer for the Government's Minor Tender Board and later for the Major Tender Board, I have broadened my understanding of suppliers, contractors, service providers, and government officer's behaviours concerning certain corrupt practices. I also underwent training on AfDB procurement procedures and the World Bank-funded Gambia Public Procurement Agency (GPPA) Act and Procurement Rules just following the setting up of GPPA. In 2007, I resigned from the civil service and registered an engineering consultancy service, called Mahfous Engineering Consultant, where on most occasions, I held procurement expert roles for locally and internationally funded projects. I am blessed to be party to numerous charity organisations e.g. Muslim Hands (UK), ISupport (UK), Shaykh Mahfous Foundation (Gambia). Since 1994, I also started and managed field offices for Muslim Hands in the Gambia, Senegal, Mali, Mauritania, at some point in time of their operations. In those years of experience, I developed a keen interest in procurement, mis-procurement, project failures, political and institutional corrupt practices, including unethical procurement processes, at the institutional and project level.

My faith as a Muslim, including a belief in the Almighty Creator and my mission to live life on a spiritual journey, has helped me find the Scale of Values. Islam teaches a complete way of life with measurable values and followers are strongly advised against corrupting them by causing corruption where it did not exist. Inculcating some of these Islamic values in my humble self and the exposure to certain corrupt practices also helped in formulating some of the phrases used here and their meaning. Naming and labelling these corrupt practices would enable societies, officials, leaders, lawmakers, academics, and the business community to study and reform these unethical, harmful practices.

My inspiration to write this book came from a LinkedIn post by Transparency International, an international organization advocating anti-corruption and transparency in a very resourceful manner. The post defined corruption in such a way that one could not see a way to enforce accountability from the vantage point and limited responsibilities held as a procurement officer. The definition emphasizes abuse of "entrusted power." Most civil servants have held the view that power lies only with the executive arm of government and not the technocrats/civil servants, since they have strict rules and guidance to follow those ranked higher. Likewise, most community organisations have established cultural norms and rules that ensure values are upheld by all in those communities. By Transparency International's definition, if you are not entrusted with power, you can't be corrupt. However, I disagree with this limited definition since corruption takes place in a variety of ways at different levels of administration.

Following a thorough review of some definitions of corruption, I came up with a universal definition that covers all forms and types of corruption following a deep reflection and study of many corruption practices. This definition would undeniably enhance the prevailing understanding of the concept of corruption, and as well become established in academic institutions to improve enacted laws and policies.

The primary objective for writing this book is to inform and prepare the young and innocent people who are at academic institutions and those who have newly joined employment in corruption-polluted governments, institutions, donor-funded projects, departments, etc, not to fall prey to the culture of corruption. With this book, they would be able to see some of the corrupt practices by presidents, prime ministers,

ministers, directors, managers, accountants, auditors, procurement officers, contracts committee members, junior and other senior staff that they may work under and be able to say no to their corrupt practices. In a corrupt working environment, it is always difficult for new employees to know that corruption is the order of the day-to-day operations as corruption in his or her workplace has become normal practice.

Moreover, I hoped, that corrupted officials within governments and other institutions would now redefine corruption to include their level of responsibility and act responsibly to add value and not cause any loss in value within their offices, projects, ministries, governments, and institutions.

This book should be helpful to policymakers and lawmakers in defining and enacting anti-corruption policies and laws. It would also help auditors have a fair understanding of the wide range of possible revenue leaks and reasons for poor project performance or failure. Audits should be extended beyond technical and financial audits and include lifestyle audits of political appointees, senior officials working at all levels of government, and funded-projects team members.

This book would also help individuals in corrupted relationships better understand themselves and start adding value to oneself and in relationships within marriage partners, family, community, and institutions. Once one finds oneself, then one begins to understand their purpose in life and invests in improving his or her human worth.

I am thankful to my mother, Sadane Mint Maline, grandmother, Mba Rohey Jammeh, Aunty Tida Bojang and John Cox, and my father Sharif Shaykh Mahfous Samsidine Hydara for the values they instilled in me. I am grateful to the Almighty Creator, Allah, for all the moments I lived and would be living through, for Islam and being a Muslim, and being in the Ummah of our beloved Prophet Muhammad, peace and blessings of Allah be upon him.

CHAPTER 2

Introduction

This book redefines corruption with an all-encompassing definition, highlighting all types and forms of corruption. It looks at a few common or well-known definitions of corruption and evaluates their limitations and effects on corrupt individuals, products, data, systems, and institutions.

The book has nine main chapters: an introduction, historical and common definitions, correct definition of corruption, causes and effects of corruption, common corrupt practices, classification of corruption, anti-corruption laws and policies, how to release oneself out of corruption, and religious statements on corruption. In short, these topics are developed and presented in a thought-provoking and self-reassessment manner.

Some of the definitions, expressions, and phrases in this book are original in nature, however, in most corrupt communities and governments the same practices and understandings may be expressed differently from how I have expressed them in this book.

This book shows that corruption is happening in different forms and degree of severity. It show how corruption occurs in human beings, between human beings, in nature, in Text and Data, in political offices, in institutions, in funded projects, communities and in countries. Considering all these forms corruptions I formulated an all-inclusive definition for corruption that should stand the test of Time.

Some of the common and standard definitions are from Internationally recognized English dictionaries and their websites. A list of websites and books are referenced.

CHAPTER 3

Historic and Common Definitions

This chapter lists a few common and historical definitions of corruption. Corruption is as old as human societies. As societies grow, they set up certain rules, values, and norms for their survival, collective growth, and progress. Most of these rules and values are derived from guidance from their Creator, Almighty God called Allah by Muslims. These values are highly protected from being corrupted by community or religious leaders. Throughout early history, it was common to kill or banish corrupted individuals from society. According to this history, human beings, religious teachings, and trading values are some of the most protected assets in early communities.

Most of the historical definitions I shall see here reflect the kind of society the writer lives in and what aspect of corruption their society was most concerned with.

Machiavelli definition. *Corruption can be defined as "the decline of virtue among political officials and the citizenry." Rephrased, this could mean ... the decline of high moral value among political officials and the citizenry.* This definition is balanced, and it considers all corrupted actors; although, it limits itself to political corruption, and does not consider other types of corruption, i.e. data and text corruption, civil servant corruption, etc.

Horst-Eberhard Richter definition. *Corruption can be defined "the undermining of political values."* This definition is too broad

it limits itself to political corruption and falls short of including other forms of corruption such as human, religious, product, etc, hence it remains limited in scope.

transparency.org definition. *"We define corruption as the abuse of entrusted power for private gain."* This definition is also limited and unbalanced. It asserts that only those entrusted with power can be corrupt. It does not consider other types of corruption, including data corruption, civil servant corruption, etc.

Investopedia definition. *"Corruption is dishonest behaviour by those in positions of power."* This definition is similarly limited and unbalanced. It asserts that only those entrusted with power can be corrupt. It does not consider the other types of corruption mentioned above.

Legaldictionary.net definition. *"The term corruption is defined as the abuse of entrusted power for personal or private gain."* This definition is also limited and unbalanced, however it includes the intent (personal gain), which is important. Yet it asserts that only those entrusted with power can be corrupt. It does not consider the other types of corruption mentioned above.

Wikipedia definition. *"Corruption is a form of dishonesty or a criminal offense which is undertaken by a person or an organization which is entrusted in a position of authority, in order to acquire illicit benefits or abuse power for one's personal gain."* Though this definition gives a bit of clarity on the intent and puts emphasis on authority and power, it is also limited. It does not consider the other types of corruption mentioned above.

All the above-mentioned definitions fail to take into consideration members of the business sector, interest groups, and lobbyists who mostly initiate bribery, buyouts, policy changes, and pocketed kickbacks, from persons entrusted with power and authority or cause other types of corruption.

CHAPTER 4

Causes and Effects of Corruption.

Some Causes of Corruption

The principal causes of corruption are evil influences from Satan, ungodliness, greed and selfishness, dishonesty, lying, the immorality of human beings, a need to be envied, or being envious of corrupted individuals.

A community will likely become corrupted if it lacks a monotheistic spiritual order, moral compass, and justice for all. A state that is poorly governed with or without anti-corruption laws, full of injustice and nepotism, low wages/salaries (earnings below the cost of basic needs), high levels of unemployment, and family dependency. Unchecked display of corrupt practices and celebrating corrupt individuals can amplify the problems of corruption.

An institution or project that is poorly planned, poorly resourced, poorly managed, and audited, with little or no accountability and transparency, no enforceable anti-corruption policy, and a high level of political interference are prone to corruption.

Some Effects of Corruption

Corruption is the main cause of most project failures, due to foot-dragging, the added cost to make up pocketed funds, religious and social ills that devalue the project, institutions, and government. Its effects on communities and/or nations are: brain drain (talent migration), inflation, unhappiness among participants or members, high unemployment rates, gang violence, drug trafficking, human trafficking, money laundering, lawlessness, lack of investment, lack of public trust, atheism, political repression, police brutality, white elephant projects, and underdevelopment of resources. These are some of the tell-all signs of corrupted communities, institutions, and governments.

CHAPTER 5

Universal Definition of Corruption

All things created can be corrupted. There are two creators: The Almighty Creator commonly known as God, Allah, and His secondary creations: human beings and their institutions. Corruption is largely practiced by humans as a part of human activities. In our World, human creators always plan, design, and produce an object or project with a specific purpose in mind. Thus, materials used in human creations go through processes and activities for a final product 'fit for purpose.'

Of all the billion or more Planets, the Almighty Creator made only Earth fit for purpose of human life to thrive, and He created human beings to live and multiply on it. The forms and shapes that the Almighty Allah gave human beings are indications that He the Almighty created us and therefore, He is our creator. Messengers and prophets are sent regularly to mankind to maintain the value of His creations and remind mankind to worship Him alone on His Earth.

All creators (humans) write either their names, or symbols, or images on all their creations e.g. Mercedes cars, or a painting by Leonardo da Vinci for people to know they are their makers. These products are unknowingly reflecting their respective makers as they profess their makers' names, present some good attributes of their makers, and become a represented image of their makers. They become, in short, a symbol of their makers. They tell the onlookers that they have a creator called company x, family y, or entrepreneur z. In effect, they bring adulation to their maker and let every onlooker know who their maker is.

The Almighty Creator, Allah, made all his creations as signs of His existence. On human Beings and living things are written Allah Almighty's signs. We humans are unknowingly continuously offering adulation toward our Creator, as we are signs, expressing His existence; we are images of His existence. We become representations of His image as some religious teachings have it "God created man in His image." It's an image (sign) expressing His existence and our ability to manifest some of His attributes.

Science has now given some insight as to what rules, measurements, and materials made Earth fit for the purpose for humans to thrive on it. The principal objective amongst many for the creation of humans is for humans to know the Almighty Creator and remember Him in worship as highlighted in most religious texts. Humans are warned by the Almighty Creator in all monotheistic religions not to cause corruption on Earth, making causing (spreading) corruption similar killing human beings. See religious texts in Chapter 10.

A human being, a product of creation, should be considered corrupt when he or she exhibits an inability to recognize the Creator, denies his or her gender for fun, worships others as gods, feeds on non-natural foods that harms his or her being, and is unable to naturally relate to people and things, etc. Human beings express and relates to others and things through their 4 states of beings. The physical self, emotional self, intellectual self and spiritual self. These can be each be corrupted and renders a person corrupted.

Nature in all it known forms becomes corrupt when it becomes polluted by human activity to a point that it becomes harmful to human being and other living things, thus rendering it useless, unfit-for-purpose, devalued, etc.

Corruption is a selfish, foolish, and greedy human act that aims to put one's own wealth or welfare above the health and proper function of an organization or relationships. It's mostly carried out by humans who lack wisdom and foresight about the negative consequences of their acts. Wisdom begins with knowing that one is a product of the Almighty Creator and knowing about the Almighty Creator and how one should relate to Him to avoid corrupting oneself and His creations. The most important foresight is to know that one will someday meet the Almighty Creator to take account of one's value. As in the case of any products, valuable ones are kept and taken care of, and useless (invaluable) are thrown away in the bin.

Humans with their godly attributes (image) naturally start secondary creations using the Almighty Creator's products. In the process, communities, towns, cities, and countries or states are created with values, rules, laws, measurements (standards), and materials (products) through projects to meet their needs. The principal objective amongst many human products and projects is human survival or convenience. Humans create products by designing, resourcing, and implementing projects, and setting up institutions that establish standards and guide the processes.

Selfishly interfering with creation processes or influencing the modification of objectives and/or altering the final product are simple acts of corruption. This interference may seem secretive, but the effects are very public since all greedy and selfish humans fondly promote and display their ill-gotten wealth or lifestyle, thus spreading corruption or the temptation to participate in corruption to others who want part of the spoils.

Corruption mostly happens between two or more humans; the corrupted and the corruptible. A corrupted human is infectious and causes loss in worth, value, or benefit of a human or project and can render a human, a thing, or a project unfit for their positive purpose. Corruption breaks social, religious, and business norms, institutional standards, ethics, and laws in social groupings and nations. It can render human beings greedy, selfish, immoral, `untrustworthy, deceitful, ungrateful, devious, envious, prideful, disloyal, dishonest, lack of integrity, addictive, infectious, criminal, and unfit for purpose.

In governments, selected leaders exploit their authority and office to enrich themselves, their families, and enablers, stealing from the commonwealth, plunging their community or district or region or state or country into underdevelopment, over debt, unattractive to investment, rampant corruption, etc., thus devaluing themselves, their office, the people they lead, and the community or district or region or state or country they rule over.

At institutions, management staff, accounting, procurement, and other junior staff enrich themselves at the cost of the institution or project they work for, leading to poor growth or total failure, project time, and cost overruns by collecting brides, kickbacks, commissions, etc.

Corruption can be synonymous with slavery. All corrupted leaders and officials become slaves to their corruptors (corrupt partners) and to their selfish desires. They lose integrity and freedom to think straight, act right, and be honest and just. Their mind is clouded like drug addicts, hindering their ability to measure failure, risk, self-value, and community or nation destruction.

A product as a secondary creation the imitates a natural product and is not fit for purpose other than profitability is corruption. Products not produced to legal standard specifications devalues the product.

Altering, and falsifying original text, message, or data to impact a people, a project, a community, or a nation for the benefit of control, financial gain, political gain or loss of values and guidance for the intended users is data or text corruption.

Corruptive practices and their effects can be identified using some of but not limited to the following criteria.

1. Infectious, negatively impacting the lives of others.
2. Selfish in motives and for gains in finances or kind.
3. Devaluing a person, thing, project, or institution.
4. Destroying a person or institution, making it unfit for its intended, positive purpose.

Based on the above criteria, I produced this all-inclusive corruption definition as follows.

Corruption is a selfish act or practice by a person or a group of people that devalues a thing or a person, an institution, or a project, which serves or would serve a group of people, a community, or a nation.

Corruption corrupts a person's mind, relationships, and body; also, products, processes, systems, data, public officers, offices, working committees, community leaders, institutions, heads of institutions, governments, ministers, and presidents.

Based on our definition, I have identified the following types of corruption.

1. Human Being Corruption.
2. Nature Corruption.
3. Political Corruption.
4. Institution/Project Corruption.
5. Product Corruption.
6. Text and Data Corruption

These are further explained in Chapter 6, Classification of Corruption

For a better understanding of our assertions in the above definition, one would need to ask a few questions as follows. Our answers to these questions attempt to give clarity by being openly broad. a) What is value? b) How does corruption devalue a person, thing, project, and institution? c) What is a project? d) What is a public office?

Value is the measurable or comparable worth of a person or thing based on its fitness for purpose at a certain time and place; a person or thing's value can be measured in terms of standards, quality, price, convenience, merit, worth, usefulness, practicality, advantage, desirability, benefit, gain, profit, good, service, helpfulness, assistance, effectiveness, efficacy, importance, significance, etc.

A person's value is a measure of:

1. quantity and quality of willful worship of the Creator,
2. virtuous deeds for mother and father
3. virtuous deeds for family, neighbors, adoptive parents, friends, community, and nation
4. the amount of time and benefits gained from oneself by other humans and living things
5. and a healthy mind and body.

Humans must be fit for purpose, hold their values dear in very high esteem, and safeguard their integrity. Human integrity is a person's quality of honesty, trustworthiness, morality, and ethical principles in a consistent manner under challenging situations.

Devalue means to cause someone or something to be less valuable or unfit for purpose or officially or legally less worthy than its previous worth. Buying a product more than its actual price devalues it for the buyer and other consumers. Paying more than the actual cost of a project devalues that project and hence devalues the institution or government implementing the project. Unknown many, business; Suppliers, Contractors and Service providers all add a *Corrupt Officer/Politician's Margin* in their real cost, hence bringing project or purchased items cost 10 to 30 percent higher than the actual cost. The corrupt individual indirectly uses a contractor or supplier to steal from very institution he or she serves.

Some examples of what devalues humans are: causing harm or loss of value (in terms of their time, assets, etc.) to other creations, worshipping something other than the Creator, lying about the truth, having a sexual relationship with another person outside of a committed acknowledged relationship, etc.

A **project** is any undertaking, conducted individually or collaboratively and possibly involving research or design, which is carefully planned to be implemented over a period and intended to achieve a particular purpose that benefits or adds value to a thing, person, community, or nation.

A Public Office is a workplace with specific functions and duties carried out by an appointed, nominated, or elected officer/officers with specific terms of reference and financial gains. By holding office, all gifts in kind or cash received from all sources belong to the office. Only a paid salary or the maximum amount permissible by policy belongs to the officer/officers. 1400 years ago, the Holy Prophet of Islam was very clear as to what the expectations of public officers should be as indicated in the Hadith below. In our opinion, this is one of the key reasons why the Islamic State was successful during and after the Prophet Mohammed's time since all public offices added value and were not selfish and greedy with public funds.

Narrated By Abu Humaid Al-Sa'idi: The Prophet Muhammed (SAWS) appointed a man from the tribe of Bani Asad, called Ibn Al-Utabiyya to collect the Zakat **(Public Office)**. *When he returned (with the money) he said (to the Prophet), "This is for you, and this has been given to me as a gift." The Prophet stood up on the pulpit (Sufyan said he ascended the pulpit), and after glorifying and praising Allah, he said, "What is wrong with the employee whom we send (to collect Zakat from the public) that he returns to say, 'This is for you and that is for me?' Why didn't he stay at his father's and mother's house to see whether he will be given gifts or not? By Him in Whose Hand my life is, whoever takes anything illegally will bring it on the Day of Resurrection by carrying it over his neck: if it is a camel, it will be grunting: if it is a cow, it will be mooing and if it is a sheep, it will be bleating!" The Prophet then raised both his hands till we saw the whiteness of his armpits (and he said), "No doubt! Haven't I conveyed Allah's Message?" And he repeated it three times.* **Sahih Bukhari Volume 9, Book 93, Hadith 7176**

CHAPTER 6

Classification of Corruption

Corruption generally is a legal crime and sinful; however, its impact and scope vary. I've identified three classes of corruption herein to express the degree and scale of corruption. These are petty corruption, severe corruption, and extreme corruption, to provide scale. This three-point scale can be used to understand and/or give an indication of the human or his community, or nation's condition in terms of corruption. See the *Sarane Classification of Corruption* table below.

In a situation where there is petty corruption, everybody is seen as having the potential to fail. Where there is severe corruption in a community or nation, institutions and projects are failing or have failed and do not have the trust of the public. Where there is extreme corruption, that community or nation is collapsing or has collapsed because members no longer can trust the institutions or their leadership to provide for their welfare. I came across a befitting description of an extremely corrupted government by Ayan Rand (American-Russian Author 1905 -1982) on Tik-Tok (CareIvanaswegen7's Account)

*"When you see that in order to produce, **you need to obtain permission from men who produce nothing;** when you see that money is flowing to those who deal not in goods, but in favors; when you see that men get rich more easily by graft than by work, and your laws no longer protect you against them but protect them against you... you may know that your society is doomed."*

Types of Corruption	Petty Corruption	Severe Corruption	Extreme Corruption	Common terminology
Environmental Corruption	• Human activity pollutant	• Industrial waste	• Nuclear explosion. • Nuclear leakages • Uranium-related weapons • Toxic waste	• **Pollution**
Data/text Corruption	• Data Misrepresentation	• Data Falsification	• Religious Text alteration	• **False Information**
Human Corruption	• Skin Bleaching • Fake Hair extensions • Tattoos • Plastic Surgery • Prostitution	• Drug Addiction • Alcohol Addiction • Polytheist • Idolatry • Criminal • Adultery • Fornication	• Transgenders • Homosexual • Gays • Lesbians • Atheists • Sexual Abuse	• **Mental/ Emotional unstable/ill**
Political Corruption	• Unnecessary travel • Unnecessary purchases • Unnecessary Projects • Unnecessary workshops	• Nepotism • Rewarding Militants/ loyalists • Extension of Office privileges to family members and friends •	• Leadership Access fees • Leadership commissions • Leadership undeclared • gifts • Leadership kickbacks •	**Abuse of Office**

		• Creation of Fake Projects/ purchases/ events • Unauthorized payouts • Missed use of Reserved Funds • lobbyist/ interest group sponsors owed	• Leadership brides • Trading in Court Cases • Executive Court Rulings • All corrupt practices listed under project corruption	
Product Corruption	• Diluting a product • Unstandardized Weights and Measures • Unbranded products	• Increase quantity by adding another product • Reduction of the standard of international products	• Complete faking of a product • Cancerous products • Poisonous products	**Fake or Substandard Products**
Project Corruption	Bribery, Cash-in On Process, Process Inducements, Kick Backs Collection, Corrupt Officer's Markup/Margin, Undeclared Gifts and Presents, Trading in Favors, Day Light Robbery, Best Price Sacrifice, Fake or False Procurement, Non-built-in Success Fees, Undeclared Commissions/Gratuity/Agent fees, Discounts owned, Ghost/Top-up Variations, Unreasonable Cost Overrun, Unreasonable Time Overrun.			**Project Failure**

Social Corruption	• Disrespectful • Petty theft	• Obscene public acts • Naked dressing • Drink Driving • Human Rights Abuse • Double Receipting • Triple Receipting • Below-standardized products/ measurement/ weights • Fake or false product certificates	• Outlaws • Feuds • Criminal gangs • Drug dealing • Apartheid • Tax Evasion	Moral Degradation

CHAPTER 7

Anti-corruption Laws, By-laws, Policies

Governments, institutions, businesses, and community-based organizations enact laws, write policies, and rules to prevent corruption and punish corrupt officials for a loss of time, revenue, and integrity due to the official's self-interest.

Most such existing documents face the challenge of correctly defining corruption; to give meaning to the intent and objectives of such documents. Existing definitions are generally specific and limited; in some cases, no definition is provided as in the case of the United Nations, World Bank, etc, where emphasis is made on impact and initiative to combat corruption.

Laws mostly focus on offenses and penalties whilst most policies are limited to less than five corrupt practices. Anti-corruption laws must not be limited to political corruption. It should include all forms of corruption, from petty to extreme, hence holding civil servants, project officials, and political appointees accountable. Audits should not be limited to financial and technical, however, it should include lifestyle audits. A lifestyle would involve a baseline audit of the individual and their immediate family's financial worth at the start of taking up office followed by random periodic reviews of the said individual during annual financial audits to uncover corrupt practices that may have increased their standard of living.

Anti-corruption policies present strategies to combat corruption, however, these strategies must include a role for the most important influencer in most people's lives; his or her belief system and the institutions that teach or administer it. There is a need to emphasize religious teaching within personal belief systems that most certainly teach values and cultivate and groom honesty. All monotheistic faiths offer guidance on anti-corruption, immorality, dishonesty, and good values in all aspects of life.

Policies must include a role for whistle-blowers, their protection, and reward. Anti-corruption policies at the government level also must include educating the citizenry from high schools up to universities on various corrupt practices and preventive measures.

However, laws and policies would all be rendered useless and or ineffective in extremely corrupt communities, institutions, or governments where corrupt politicians, civil servants, and officials oversee, manage, and are also accountable for those organizations. 'A-Few-Good-Men-Standing' could be better than any of these legal instruments in such environments. The media and civil societies should endeavour to support and enhance the activities of groups or individuals standing up against corruption.

Countries that want to zero-in on corruption should work close with international CSOs like Transparency International, make good use of their resources and work towards improving their ranking.

CHAPTER 8

Some Common Corrupt Practices

In this chapter, I came up with a definition of the most known corrupt practices and many common practices that are not regularly known or named. These newly named corrupted practices in this book should find their way into anti-corruption laws and policies of institutions and governments.

Adultery/fornication. These are the living conditions of corrupted minds addicted to a neighbor/friend/relative's wife or neighbor/friend/relative's daughter for sexual satisfaction.

Alcohol/Drug addiction. A living condition of a corrupted mind that loses his/her sense of purpose in life and hinders their ability to measure failure, risk, self-value, and community or nation destruction.

Atheism. A living condition of a corrupted mind's self-denial of his or her Creator's existence partly due to his inability to believe or perhaps a negative experience with corrupt religious person or institutions in their past.

Best Price Sacrifice. When an employee, usually a procurement officer or accounts staff or a procurement/contract committee or public officer with the authority to approve or disapprove a decision or the authority to supervise a process agrees to award a contract to a responsive bidder with a higher price on condition that that bidder shares the difference in cost between his/her price and the responsive lowest price or they ask for a discount as a condition for the award of a contract and ask that the discount be paid to them in cash.

Bribery. An act of giving in-kind rewards or cash to a public officer/ officer with the hope that it would influence their decision in your favor for a vested interest in that public office or against an illegal act committed. Equally, it is the act of receiving/benefitting from a supplier/ contractor or their agents or public infrastructure user in-kind or cash because of one's position in a public office.

Cash-in On Process. The act of requesting/receiving/benefitting in cash or kind from a winning supplier/contractor by a committee or a committee member or public officer with authority to approve or disapprove a decision or authority to supervise a process; by giving the impression or asserting that said supplier/contractor would be awarded a contract due to his or her input in the process.

Contract Scope Exploitation. A practice where a contract scope is altered or reduced to save costs to compensate a contractor, supplier, or service provider for kickbacks and bribes given out to the client or its representative. The said contract would still be paid in full.

Corrupt Politician/Officer's Markup/Margin. An amount of money added to the final cost of a product or project to ensure that a supplier/contractor does not lose its anticipated profit doing business in a corrupted society and government or with a corrupted politician/officer or institution.

Data or Text Alteration. The act of altering, and falsifying original text, message, or data to impact a people, a project, a community, or a nation for the benefit of control, financial gain, political gain or loss of values and guidance for the intended users.

Hazardous litter. The act of dumping toxic or non-decomposable materials within or around human and other creatures' environment.

Day Light Robbery. An employee, usually a procurement officer, an accounts staff, or a procurement/contract committee member who uses a business entity or its agent to steal from the organization, business, or government. They secure a contract through a 3 quotations

'RFQ' or selective single-phase procurement process. Identifies the winner for the tender before the process starts and instructs the identified winner to add a certain sum for them and ensures his or her price is the lowest. The identified winner would be free to select his or her competitors who would agree at a cost to loose the bid/tender.

Discounts owned. An employee, usually a procurement officer or accounts staff or a procurement/contract committee requests a discount in cash from a supplier/contractor/service provider and does not discount it on the payment receipt or contract nor declare it to the employer and collects the discount from supplier/contractor/service provider for his or her or their personal use.

Double Receipting. Revenue collectors work with their superiors to have double receipt/ticket books with the same numbering; a set of books for the institution they work for and the other set for themselves.

Executive Court Rulings: The President of a Country, a Minister of Justice, or a Chief Justice directs the outcome of a court case before the hearing begins for personal or political gains.

Fake or False Procurement. Teamwork by officials (contracts committee members, accounting officers, head of stores or works supervisor) at an institution or Government Ministry/Department agrees with a supplier/contractor to respond to an RFQ with three quotations (his plus two others from suppliers/contractors who owed him favors or are paid off) for product/services/works that do not exist and procuring organization award him the contract, fakes the delivery of goods/services/works and pays the suppliers/contractor, who then shares the money between them.

Fake or False Product. The act of modifying genes of a living thing for financial gains at the detriment of humans benefitting from feeding on them. The process of printing food for human consumption. Production of poor quality and less durable things and claims the opposite.

Ghost Variations. These are fake variations created on paper and paid for by clients to cover unexpected financial requests from a client or its representatives to a contractor/supplier. The request mostly comes just after contract signing and advance payment is affected or before an important political or social event. After making such cash payments, the contractor or supplier or services provider would agree with the client to create a Ghost Variation to cover their loss.

Homosexualism. A living condition of a corrupted mind's self-denial of his emotional self's functional purpose in life. They read and want their kind, spend time and resources on them, and one of them role-plays a woman's life.

Idolatry/Worshipping other than the Creator. A living condition of a corrupted mind that denies his/her Creator willful worship and willfully worships the Creator's creations.

Kick Backs Collection. The act by a committee or a committee member or public officer with the authority to approve or disapprove a decision or the authority to supervise a process; receiving/benefitting from an ongoing project or completed projects or transactions by asking cash or kind from supplier/contractors or their agents.

Lesbianism. A living condition of a corrupted mind's self-denial of her emotional self's functional purpose in life. They read and want their kind, spend time and resources on them, and one of them role-plays a man's life.

Non-built-in Success Fees. An amount or percent of a contract/investment sum requested by a procuring organization or its agents for successfully signing a contract with a supplier or contractor.

Non-standard weights and measurements. The use of non-standard weights and measurements in sales or quality control to make more profit or meet basic costs by tampering or interfering, or altering standard weights and measurements, or using non-calibrated weights and measurements.

Obscene Acts in Public. The mindset of dressing half naked or fully naked or satisfying your sexual desire in a public setting where the people around have not expressed similarly.

Pre-bid Contract Award. The client, consultant, contractor, or supplier prepares a shortlist of favored trading partners and agrees on who would be the winner of a tender before the bidding process. They also agree on a profit margin percentage to be added for all the other bidders, who then bid higher than the agreed winner.

Process Inducement. The act by suppliers/contractors, or their agents, giving cash or kind to a committee or a committee member or public officer with authority to approve or disapprove a decision or authority to supervise a process to fast track or give preference of time or action at the detriment of competitors.

Trading in Court Cases. Legal luminaires such as solicitors, lawyers, and prosecutors or judges make deals for personal gains on a) the outcome of a court case, b) unnecessarily prolonging a case to outrun the plaintiff's patience, and c) agreeing with a high-profile client's lawyer to lose a case against his/her client.

Trading in Favors. Receiving and/or returning favors to individuals, businesses, or interest groups, against policies at the detriment of the institution/company/government the receiver works for.

Triple Receipting. Revenue collectors work with their superiors to have two receipt/ticket books with the same numbering, however, he or she adds a third book with the same numbering; a set of books for the institution they work for, the other set for themselves, and a third set for himself or herself.

Undeclared Commissions/Gratuity/Agent fees. These fees must be inscribed in agreements/contracts and requisite services performed before payment. Different organizations have policies for such fees and set limits to the amounts. Undeclared such fees are corruption (extortion and unreasonable kickbacks).

Undeclared Gifts and Presents. Receiving gifts and presents from individuals, businesses, and interest groups valued beyond acceptable values stipulated in government or company policies on gifts and presents.

CHAPTER 9

Find Yourself Out of Corrupt Relations

To combat corrupt practices within and around oneself, one must know oneself, find oneself, and take control of oneself. The human being project is a long-term project that requires focus, knowledge, wisdom (experience), well-being, and patience for its success. The human being has a physical self, an intellectual self, an emotional self, and a spiritual self. These can all be corrupted, rendering the human being corruptly relating to others and things thus living a corruption relationship.

The physical being works through time with energy and knowledge, the intellectual being expresses the knowable after recollecting the known, the emotional being attaches and detaches in joy and pain, and the spiritual being carries the burden of the other three 'beings' including sensitivity to corrupt practices and value-added practices.

Knowing how one relates to others and things helps in one knowing oneself. You are the values you live by and relate positively to things through your needs, wants, likes, and love. For example, a woman needs a husband, wants to be a good wife, and loves her children, the Creator, prophets, saints and all good people. For a better understanding of oneself, one must be clear about things that are of need, of want, of like, and of love, hence one would become known to oneself. To 'Like' requires no reasoning, it is momentary, undervaluing, and a non-complimentary effort when used for humans and most things. Its suitable for the individual five human sense's response to things. As for love, it's a matter of the heart and is for the Creator and His high-value creations.

Mixing these relationships shows one state of being. In the poem below, I try to show the different attitudes influenced by the wrong application of these words in one's life.

Know Yourself

Know what are of needs

And know your needs

Know what are of wants

And know your wants

Know what are of likes

And know what looks like you

Need not what you want.

Want not what you need.

Need not what you like.

Like not what you need.

Want not what you like.

Like not what you want.

When your needs become wants, you become arrogant.

When your needs become likes, you become ungrateful.

When your wants become needs, you become greedy.

When your wants become likes, you become corrupt.

When your likes become needs, you become an addict.

When your likes become wants, you become selfish.

The negative attributes mentioned above are hallmarks of a corrupt individual. Fighting personal corrupt practices is a self-seeking uphill task that requires continuous self-assessment and monitoring.

To assist one in the process of finding oneself, I have created a game 'Sharif Forbidden Words Game'. The game enhances thought processes and language. I found the English language to be one of the most spiritual languages in the unintended worship of the Almighty Creator Allah or God. Those who know, know that the English language casually use the letters of the secret great name of the Israel Almighty God and some sounds of the secret greatest name of the Muslim Almighty God. All English-speaking human beings unknowingly worship their Creator, hence the reason, in my opinion for it being spoken all over the world as the dominant language of Humanity. However, the English language has certain words that seem to cast negative spells on human behaviour and can cause corruption in human relations, affecting the regular user's lifestyles, duties, and responsibilities.

I have identified a few such words and advise all those who want to contribute positively to their life, family, institution, community, state, or country to remove them from their thought process and speech in all their relationships with humans and all things. In these circles, teamwork, respect, trust, honesty, sincerity, and integrity become very important. Here are a few of such words; I, But, Like, Fun, Problem, and Boring. Fun is for children not even for teenagers much more adults. One's choice of certain words can indicate one's state of being and removal of certain words from one's choice of words would drastically change one's state of being. In the poem below I try to explain why these words spell out negative energy.

<u>Sharif Forbidden Words</u>

I don't work with a team.

Selfishness lives in I

I don't contribute to We-interest.

But the worst listener.

Agrees without Buts

Since But is never sincere.

Like similar to ungratefulness

Unknowing arrogantly Likes.

As Like denies beauty it's due.

Fun hollowed and empty.

The unfocused full of Fun.

As Fun builds houses of regrets

Problem is not real.

Difficulties are solutions to Problems.

As Problems shuts solutions out.
Boring is focusing on details.
Creative minds are never bored.
Boring is not progressive.

This game can be played in friendships, partnerships, family homes, all communal events, gatherings, camping events, project teamwork, business environments, and office environments where teamwork is required. Some of these words have better alternatives, players can come up with alternatives that would help bring out the positive team energy required in completing tasks. Individuals who hold leadership positions and remove such negative words, in thought processes and expressions, would demonstrate high leadership quality in gatherings. For singles seeking partners for marriage or those already married and having difficulties maintaining a married life, this game could help positively change the mindset to help one live a successful married life.

The game has two rules. Rule 1. All participants agree to omit these words in their thought process and speech and accept any reminders from other participants when they use any of the listed words above Rule 2. All participants should always remind themselves and others not to use these words when they use anyone of them.

CHAPTER 10

Religious Verses on Corruption

This chapter lists a few religious texts on corruption as a reminder for religious readers and an exposure for non-religious readers. I am not a religious scholar, however by listing these texts, I am expressing their importance in one's struggle out of corruption, corrupt relationships and being.

Virtue, morality, ethics, good behaviour, etc are all thoroughly taught by religious texts and religious leaders who groom their followers to be high-valued creations. The Creator has constantly and regularly sent messengers and prophets to humanity to teach how to willingly worship Him, with reminders on how to live an uncorrupted life. Only the monotheistic religions refer to the Creator as their source of guidance, hence I herein present a few verses on corruption from monotheistic religious books as a reminder for those with faith who still live a corrupted life.

Al Quran Kareem This is the Holy Book or Scripture of Muslims. It lays down for them the law and commandments, codes for their social and moral behaviour, and contains a comprehensive religious [spirituality and] philosophy.

Hadith/Ahadith is the record of the words, actions, and approvals teachings of Prophet Muhammad (Peace be upon him) as transmitted through chains of narrators. Pious Muslims must do their utmost to live life in a way exemplary of the Prophet through these teachings.

The Holy Bible is a collection of religious texts or scriptures, some, all, or a variant of which are held to be sacred in Christianity, Judaism, Samaritanism, Islam, the Baha'i Faith, and many other Abrahamic religions.

THE HOLY QURAN Aisha Bewley. Translation

1. *Al Quran Chapter 30 [30:41]*

Corruption has appeared throughout the land and sea by [reason of] what the hands of people have earned so He may let them taste part of [the consequence of] what they have done that perhaps they will return [to righteousness].

1. *Al Quran Chapter 2 [2:11]*

When they are told, 'Do not cause corruption on the earth,' they say, 'We are only putting things right.'

1. *Al Quran Chapter 2 [2:27]*

Those who break Allah's contract after it has been agreed, and sever what Allah has commanded to be joined, and cause corruption on the earth, it is they who are the lost.

1. *Al Quran Chapter 2 [2:30]*

When your Lord said to the angels, 'I am putting a khalif on the earth,' they said, 'Why put on it one who will cause corruption on it and shed blood when we glorify You with praise and proclaim Your purity?' He said, 'I know what you do not know.'

1. *Al Quran Chapter 2 [2:205]*

When he leaves you, he goes about the earth corrupting it, destroying crops and animals. Allah does not love corruption.

1. <u>*Al Quran Chapter 5 [5:32]*</u>

on account of that. So, We decreed for the tribe of Israel that if someone kills another person – unless it is in retaliation for someone else or for causing corruption in the earth – it is as if he had murdered all mankind. And if anyone gives life to another person, it is as if he had given life to all mankind. Our Messengers came to them with Clear Signs but even after that many of them committed outrages in the earth.

1. <u>*Al Quran Chapter 7 [7:85]*</u>

And to Madyan We sent their brother Shu'ayb who said, 'My people, worship Allah! You have no other god than Him. A Clear Sign has come to you from your Lord. Give full measure and full weight. Do not diminish people's goods. Do not cause corruption in the land after it has been put right. That is better for you if you are muminun.

1. <u>*Al Quran Chapter 7 [7:127]*</u>

The ruling circle of Pharaoh's people said, 'Are you going to leave Musa and his people to cause corruption in the earth and abandon you and your gods?' He said, 'We will kill their sons and let their women live. We have absolute power over them!'

1. <u>*Al Quran Chapter 8 [8:73]*</u>

Those who are kafir are the friends and protectors of one another. If you do not act in this way, there will be turmoil in the land and great corruption.

1. *Al Quran Chapter 11 [11:116]*

Would that there had been more people with a vestige of good among the generations of those who came before you, who forbade corruption in the earth, other than the few among them whom We saved. Those who did wrong gladly pursued the life of luxury that they were given and were evildoers.

1. *Al Quran Chapter 13 [13:25]*

But as for those who break Allah's contract after it has been agreed and sever what Allah has commanded to be joined, and cause corruption in the earth, the curse will be upon them. They will have the Evil Abode.

AHADITH – SAYINGS AND WAY OF LIFE OF MUHAMMAD (Peace be upon him)

1. *Hadith – Al Muwatta Imam Malik*

Malik related to me that he heard that Abdullah ibn Masud used to say, "You must tell the truth. Truthfulness leads to right action. Right action leads to the Garden. Beware of lying. Lying leads to corruption, and corruption leads to the Fire. Don't you see that it is said, 'He speaks the truth and acts rightly,' and 'He lies and is corrupt.' "

1. *Hadith – **Sunan Abu Dawood:***

Narrated Abu Hurairah: The Prophet said: "If anyone corrupts (instigates) the wife of a man or his slave (against him), he is not from us."

Narrated Miqdam ibn Madikarib and Abu Umamah: The Prophet said: "When a ruler seeks to make imputations against the people, he corrupts them."

'Arfajah reported that the Prophet said: "Various corruptions will arise in my community, so strike with the sword the one who tries to cause separation in the matter of Muslims when they are united, whoever he..."

1. *Hadith – Muwatta Malik*

Yahya related to me from Malik from Yahya ibn Said that Muadh ibn Jabal said, "There are two military expeditions. There is one military expedition in which valuables are spent, the contributor is willing, the authorities are obeyed, and corruption *is avoided. That military expedition is all good. There is a military expedition in which valuables are not spent, the contributor is not willing, the authorities are not obeyed, and* corruption *is not avoided. The one who fights in that military expedition does not return with reward."*

1. *Hadith – Sunan Abi Dawud*

Narrated Abu Hurayrah:
The Prophet (saws) said: If anyone corrupts *(instigates) the wife of a man or his slave (against him), he is not from us.*

1. *Hadith – Sunan Abi Dawud*

Narrated Miqdam ibn Ma'dikarib; AbuUmamah:
The Prophet (saws) said: When a ruler seeks to make imputations against the people, he corrupts *them.*

1. *Hadith – Al-Adab Al-Mufrad*

Abu Hurayra reported that the Messenger of Allah, may Allah bless him and grant him peace, said, "The believer is guileless and generous while the corrupt *is a swindler and miserly."*

1. *Hadith – Mishkat al-Masabih*

'Arfaja told that he heard God's Messenger say, "Various corruptions will arise, so strike with the sword him who tries to cause separation in this people when they are united, whoever he be." Muslim transmitted it.

1. *Hadith – Mishkat al-Masabih*

An-Nu'man b. Bashir reported God's Messenger as saying, "What is lawful is clear and what is unlawful is clear, but between them are certain doubtful things which many people do not recognize. He who guards against doubtful things keeps his religion and his honour blameless, but he who falls into doubtful things falls into what is unlawful, just as a shepherd who pastures his animals round a preserve will soon pasture them in it. Every king has a preserve, and God's preserve is the things He has declared unlawful. In the body there is a piece of flesh, and the whole body is sound if it is sound, but the whole body is corrupt if it is corrupt. It is the heart." (Bukhari and Muslim.)

1. *Hadith – Mishkat al-Masabih*

He reported God's Messenger as saying, "When someone with whose religion and character you are satisfied asks your daughter in marriage, accede to his request. If you do not do so there will be temptation in the earth and extensive corruption." Tirmidhi transmitted it.

1. *Hadith – Sunan Abi Dawud*

'Arfajah told that he heard the Messenger of Allah (May peace be upon him) as saying; various corruptions will arise in my community, so strike with sword the one who tries to cause separation in the matter of Muslims when they are united, whoever he be.

'Ali reported God's messenger as saying, "A time is soon coming to mankind when nothing of Islam, but its name will remain and only the written form of the Qur'an will remain. Their mosques will be in fine condition but will be devoid of guidance, their learned men will be the worst people under heaven, corruption coming forth from them and returning among them." Baihaqi transmitted it in Shu'ab al-iman.

THE HOLY BIBLE – *Books of Jewish and Christian Prophets*
King James Version

1. *Psalms Chapter 53*

The fool hath said in his heart, there is no God. Corrupt are they and have done abominable iniquity: there is none that doeth good.

1. *Acts 13:37*

But he, whom God raised again, saw no corruption.

1. *Psalms 49:9*

That he should still live forever, and not see corruption.

1. *Acts 13:35*

Wherefore he saith also in another psalm, thou shalt not suffer thine Holy One to see corruption.

1. *1 Corinthians 15:42*

So also, is the resurrection of the dead. It is sown in corruption; it is raised in corruption:

1. *1 Corinthians 15:50*

Now this I say, brethren, that flesh and blood cannot inherit the king-dom of God; neither doth corruption inherit in corruption.

1. *Acts 2:31*

He seeing this before spake of the resurrection of Christ, that his soul was not left in hell, neither his flesh did see corruption.

1. *Psalms 16:10*

For thou wilt not leave my soul in hell; neither wilt thou suffer thine Holy One to see corruption.

1. *Acts 2:27*

Because thou wilt not leave my soul in hell, neither wilt thou suffer thine Holy One to see corruption.

1. *Romans 8:21*

Because the creature itself also shall be delivered from the bondage of corruption into the glorious liberty of the children of God.

1. *Acts 13:34*

And as concerning that he raised him up from the dead, now no more to return to corruption, he said on this wise, I will give you the sure mercies of David.

1. *2 Peter 2:19*

While they promise them liberty, they themselves are the servants of corruption: for of whom a man is overcome, of the same is he brought in bondage.

1. *2 Peter 2:12*

But these, as natural brute beasts, made to be taken and destroyed, speak evil of the things that they understand not; and shall utterly perish in their own corruption.

1. *Acts 13:36*

For David, after he had served his own generation by the will of God, fell on sleep, and was laid unto his fathers, and saw corruption:

1. *Jonah 2:6*

I went down to the bottoms of the mountains; the earth with her bars was about me forever: yet hast thou brought up my life from corruption, O LORD my God.

1. *Leviticus 22:25*

Neither from a stranger's hand shall ye offer the bread of your God of any of these; because their corruption is in them, and blemishes be in them: they shall not be accepted for you.

1. *2 Peter 1:4*

Whereby are given unto us exceeding great and precious promises: that by these ye might be partakers of the divine nature, having escaped the corruption that is in the world through lust.

1. *Isaiah 38:17*

Behold, for peace I had great bitterness: but thou hast in love to my soul delivered it from the pit of corruption: for thou hast cast all my sins behind thy back.

1. *Daniel 10:8*

Therefore, I was left alone, and saw this great vision, and there remained no strength in me: for my comeliness was turned in me into corruption, and I retained no strength.

1. *Galatians 6:8*

For he that soweth to his flesh shall of the flesh reap corruption; but he that soweth to the Spirit shall of the Spirit reap life everlasting.

1. *2 Kings 23:13*

And the high places that were before Jerusalem, which were on the right hand of the mount of corruption, which Solomon the king of Israel had built for Ashtoreth the abomination of the Zidonians, and for Chemosh the abomination of the Moabites, and for Milcom the abomination of the children of Ammon, did the king defile.

CHAPTER 11

Reference

1 https://www.transparency.org/en/what-is-corruption

2 www.wikipedia.org

3 https://www.investopedia.com/terms/c/corruption.asp

4 https://www.unodc.org/corruption/en/learn/what-is-corruption.html

5 https://legaldictionary.net/corruption/

6 https://en.wikipedia.org/wiki/Political_corruption

7 https://nawatch.org/wp-content/uploads/2024/06/The-Gambia-Anti-Corruption-Bill-2019-Final.pdf,

8 www.alislam.org

9 www.haramiweb.com

10 Gambia Anti-corruption Bill 2019

11 https://dictionary.cambridge.org/dictionary/english/corrupt

12 https://www.merriam-webster.com/dictionary/corrupt

13 https://www.collinsdictionary.com/dictionary/english/corrupt

14 Webster's New World Dictionary – Modern Curriculum Press; Revised Basic

School Edition – ISBN 0–8136-1997-1

15 https://www.dictionary.com.

16 https://dictionary.cambridge.org,

17 https://www.collinsdictionary.com,

18 https://www.vocabulary.com,

19 https://www.britannica.com.

20 https://www.ldoceonline,
21 https://oboloo.com,
22 https://www.ethicssage.com,
23 https://www.macmillandictionary.com
24 https://www.investopedia.com ,
25 https://www.oxfordlearnersdictionaries.com
26 https://www.thesaurus.com
27 https://en.wiktionary.org
28 https://www.jstor.org
29 https://publications.iadb.org
30 https://www.elibrary.imf.org
31 https://www.verywellmind.com
32 https://corporatefinanceinstitute.com
33 https://andrewreeves.co.uk
34 https://www.simplilearn.com
35 https://www.pmi.org
36 https://www.wrike.com
37 https://www.projectmanager.com
38 https://www.apm.org.uk
39 https://www.managementstudyguide.com
40 https://www.yourdictionary.com

Index

Printed in the USA
CPSIA information can be obtained
at www.ICGtesting.com
CBHW010706241124
17860CB00074B/1390